mermaid lungs

jasmine s. higgins

mermaid lungs

jasmine s. higgins

Contents

life is so silly
so utterly pointless
but for whatever reason
i continue
to try to matter

small and pointless

we exist for a moment
and the universe doesn't notice

maybe it blinks
misses the whole of humanity
earth's temperature rises
big sigh as she rolls over in her sleep
a gazillion lights and footsteps
and then we're extinct

and briefly
the small green thing
looked a little less green
vibrated with laughter
littered with tiny breathing things
but it's over now
and the earth rests easier
now the itch of us
has been scratched

life is so silly
so utterly pointless
but for whatever reason
i continue
to try to matter
and so this is me trying
to tell you what i'm worth
with my little human words
and hoping someone
will believe me

i am a misplaced thing

i want to make my bed
and lay my head
in a new town every night
and i want to stay
in my childhood bedroom

                              forever

i want to be in the middle of nowhere
and never be perceived
i want to be in a big loud city
and i want human beings

                    to look at me

i want to be alone
and i want to be known
i want it all
without anyone needing me
tell me i'm worth more
than this town
tell me i'm more

                    than this city

maybe i'm a drifting soul
and i don't know how to be

but maybe nothing feels like home
when you're 23

vanity

or is it just
an aching to know
what it means to exist?

i miss myself
every time
i turn out the light
is it vanity?

or fear of facing
myself in the dark
rid of eyes, skin, costume
just the invisible
the ugly
the always there

is it vanity
to think of myself at all?
aware i exist
worried i'm doing it wrong
hoping i'll be okay

is it vanity?
it can't be,
can it?

breaking point

this is how it ends:
i tell you i love you
and the world dissolves on god's tongue
we can't go on like this, and if we can't, nothing can

this is how we'll be remembered:
we won't
but does it matter?
i can feel you on my skin, in my chest
but we were only ever meant to fade

this is how it burns:
like a volcano
like a room full of dust
like an accident we both saw coming
but had too much pride to prevent
(we've all seen the news)

this is where i run:
straight for the sea
for the world that isn't the world
my end was always going to be
at the hands of you
sordid sun
i can't bring myself
to look at you anymore
i just can't
so i'm staying in the deep wet dark
until you find something else
to burn

you're not the world anymore

how did the sky look
the moment we broke?
my eyes on you,
my life held loosely
in your uninterested hands

freedom with the sweet taste
as you walked away
you knew i was at the window
looking at you

and you never turned back
you had a world full of things to love
and i hummed like white noise behind you

instead
you were looking at the sky
holy everything
endless blue
and i missed it for you

the world as it stood
clouds holding each other as we let go
how everything   begins and ends,
   begins and ends   and our ending
was so many beginnings

i looked at you
because i thought you were it

and that'll teach me
not to gaze out the window
with the intention of looking down
instead of up

i can't believe the way

my lungs settle for air that doesn't contain you
and i gave in and washed the last clothes
you would ever touch me in
because they simply needed to be washed
and it was no use holding onto fragments
that would fade anyway

i can't believe the mattress in my old flat
that learnt your heartbeat the way it learnt mine
still exists
and someone who will never know our names
sleeps on it
the bed that was once my bed is now
a stranger's bed

and the worst part is it doesn't matter
it doesn't matter
that the place where we were us is still standing
because we're not us anymore
we're just not
that was then and this is now
we could stand wrapped around each other
on that road and talk about uni and being 21
but it wouldn't take us back

what we are now
is a pair of half-hearts that don't match
occasionally flirting like nothing ever went wrong
just to feel young
and other nights
sharing our existential dread

you told me you're turning 25 this year
i reminded you you were 22 when we met
and you said *oh god, don't say that*

i can't bear the weight of knowing
how much i will resent myself in the future
when i look back and see that i spent my youth
mourning my youth

but my god
it hurts to grow up
i hear a dreadful dance hit from 2016
and it makes me ache

the sound of being just old enough
to start having fun on my own terms
but really
still being a kid
drinking the blue stuff
smoking skinny cigarettes
singing to strangers

because everyone in a night club
who isn't 18
hates everyone there who is 18
so why would you bother trying
to be anything better

you tell me in your head you're just 16
you feel like your first holiday with friends
just happened

and in one of the clouds in my mind
i am sitting on the pavement
just off prince of wales road
with a handful of cheesy chips
laughing with two of my favourite people
about the good old days
that had only just happened
reminiscing on the previous year
like it was a lifetime ago

now that 2am spent with them
feels like yesterday
but it's been four years
and i never see them anymore

if you and i had met 100 years ago
like this, in our twenties
i think we would've gotten married
i think we had something special
maybe not special enough for this lifetime
but more than i'd have wished for
in any other

i can't bear the growing distance between us
between now and then
how we're rushed and pushed
to grow into a life where we can settle
like real grown ups
and how this process is pulling us apart
instead of together

it kills me that we weren't made for each other
and that life was so cruel
to make me think we were

but just like i'll never forget my 2am
laughing with an ex
turned forever friend
and you'll never forget the summer
when everyone you knew
was on the same island
just like we have these memories of youth
times that felt like magic then
and feel no less special now
we will always have our october

someday beloved

lover, when
will i find you?
do you know that i
am out here
searching?
have we met?
that would be so typical

i feel our love already
is that strange?
like i know
we will exist
like our love
is waiting
maturing in a cave
like cheddar
or gouda

will you love the way
i make everything
about cheese?
oh, i don't know
will you love me
at all?

new lust

your breath softens like spring rain
sunrise glistening on the thames
i learn your words at 3am
and you love the way i say your name

like within it
there are things to find
and i intend to find them

in this sacred town
of sweet delights and growing pains
you learn my poems and yet
you still don't know me at all

and that is the best thing

bare skin

your lips
how they always find a home
pressed to my shoulder
nudges you to wake up
you're missing the good bit
television rolls its eyes
look into mine, moving closer
to the blurring point
out the freckle on my wrist
held above my head
resting on your shoulder
face against bare skin
and i can't help
but kiss it

all that glows

in this town the nights are bright
streetlights and ever-glowing signs
dance through my window so i know
it's never the wrong time to be awake

flashing colours mixed with sounds
of cars beeping and people laughing
or crying or fighting
always existing

streets always vibrant no matter the hour
and you, and us, we're no different
giggling at little nothings through the night
wandering by the river in sweet midday

in the lukewarm light of early march
or the buzzing glow of my old tv
we're golden, neon, and everything in between
every living thing is a light in its own right

and every hold of my hand is a spring afternoon
and every kiss is midnight

pressed against the cold wet road
feeling for its pulse
all i want is to be seen

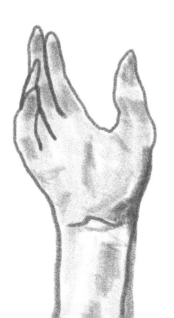

march, 2020

three days took six months to pass

bodies splayed the way they do
when they sleep alone

i cried for you

love before lockdown

it started with wine
nervous voices, real smiles
the usual jokes about our favourite shows
that we're not used to telling each other
finding common ground is like finding dust masks
in the hardware store (before all of this happened)
always possible, but tedious

it started with sitting side by side
wondering why our hands weren't touching

bodies holding each other at night
settling into each other's breath
fidgeting, rolling away
coming right back
nestling into safe arms

it started with three months left
before i leave this town
enough time to fall in love or out of it
and decide if we'd be worth a longer drive
we've got time to have fun
we can talk about that when the time comes

i'm leaving to stay safe
but i'll be back in a week
i'll see you soon, okay?
three months, we've got time
don't miss me too much

and then it stopped

spider poem #1

deirdre, i don't mind
that you don't pay rent

that you massacre the flies in my bedroom
and drop their hollow bodies onto my bed
that i find fractured wings in my morning hair
and sprinkles of broken limbs between my pillows

i don't mind the buzzing screams
just as i am falling asleep

you help me make the most of a bad thing
in this new life
i need routine
and i know it's time for bed
when the murder begins
i lay here watching
as you begin to feast
and i wish my obsessions
didn't all involve dead things
but here we are

spider living above my bed,
i'm glad you're with me

drunk girls screaming outside my house at 4am

torches hunting in the dark
like moon-sized lasers
blazing through the black
spring air through opened windows
i peek to see what is happening

on the edge of the green
screaming like no one has ever
told them not to
laughing like the world is not
what it has become
howling at the sky like they belong

three drunk girls in the road
trying to roll one cigarette between them
six hands and no success
they play until it breaks
'where even are we?'
the dogs start to bark
and the girls bark back
'can you believe we have to go home
in five hours?'
'i don't want to go home'
and so they scream some more

how strange
for anyone to be out at all
in the unbearable late-night frost
let alone in lockdown

to be in no hurry to leave
and go home where it's warm

and of course i resent them
for waking me at this hour
in my house
that belongs to no town
where no one ever passes
but my god, i ache
for teenagers living all their teenage pain
stuck indoors every day
of course they don't want to go home

although i'm distressed by their shouting
and angry beyond words
that they upset my dogs
i am grateful to have heard voices for once
they brought chaos to a place
where nothing ever happens

i hope they got home safe

insomniac's dawn

rattle me
with panic and sadness and grief
shake me out of my sleep
turn me into a haunted house
broken windows, crooked beams

watch me lie awake
in the shivering ache of 4am
desperate for the light to come
for the birds to sing
so i can stop forcing sleep

the chickens begin to rise
softly clucking into 5am
waking each other gently
into a day so peaceful
like all of their days
roaming through the trees
and all of life's goodness

i feel distress in the dark hours
guilt for my open eyes
in a time of rest
but relief comes
with the day's beginning
for when morning is here
and it is time to wake
i am already winning

bee's forbidden fruit

spring aura
tempts me with its yellow hues
buttercup blooms and sweet sunshine
gentle breeze sways the grass
and i am desperate
to touch it
to press honeysuckle to my tongue
my tongue
pressed
against the glass
my wings ache but i cannot stop
i will not stop
until i taste that world
if only someone
would open the window

if you knew how to love me

would you do it?
would you fall into me
heart wide-open
smiling like you've won
every minute grateful
that you saw the light?

would you dip your toes in
the waters of my chest
fingers in my hair
feeling around curiously
wondering what it is
that my body holds
and if it's worth drowning for?

would you run barefoot
like the building is burning
my body a sinking ship
like if you let yourself love
you'd be breaking too?

would you shrug
because you've been here already
you've loved me before
and you could do it again
am i silly to think
you don't know how to love me

when perhaps the truth is
i'm just a love you know how
to walk away from?

city sounds

i close my eyes
and i picture london
high heels on pavements
sweaty buses and tubes
pigeons with more confidence
than i will ever have

i picture the lush store at liverpool street
bright and buzzing as always
sometimes i'd stop by there
on my way through london
to buy something, or just to chat
what a horrifying place
when you're feeling antisocial
but what a lifesaving place
when you need someone
to smile at you and say hello

i picture oxford street
the way it looked the first time i went
how terrifying
the primark was filled with more people
than i knew to exist in the world

and i picture my road
noisy at all hours
a lullaby to my peaceless mind
inviting my insomnia out of guilt

i picture london how i left it
because i can't bear the thought
of it ever being anything else
i listen to street noises
on youtube to fall asleep
and i tell myself that london
has not stopped

and this lie is all that gets me
through the night

between sheets

foetal creatures, curled up tight
nestled in warmth and safety

even at 80
our sheets imitate the womb every night
we rest the way we did
before we knew anything else

        fall into unconsciousness
                like we've never met the world

each day you read the news
and each night your desperation grows
for a deep, heavy sleep
to carry it all away
still the morning comes
and the news tells you it has, in fact,
gotten worse
after yesterday you swore it couldn't

but each morning we are new
we are reborn
into a day that may be worse
than the ones before
but is undoubtedly closer
to the day where it gets better

and we will be reborn
on that day, too

i miss bookshops

i miss strangers handing me a book
and saying 'read this, it made me cry'
buying it because how could i not
if it meant so much to someone
that they couldn't help but place it
in my hands

i miss the old man behind the counter
nodding in approval at my choices
'leonard cohen, very nice' he would say
and i'd smile back at him

i miss how book people love other book people
how everyone in that shop looked at me
like i was one of them

they didn't care that i didn't read a single book
for four years as a teenager
that i've hardly read any classics
and i read so slow
that i've forgotten the beginning
by the time i reach the end

every time someone walked into that shop
every time i spotted someone on the train
with jane austen in hand
in a sea of airpods
i felt known, i felt seen

so in isolation, i suppose
i should just keep reading

spider poem #2

deirdre, did you know
there is a blizzard
frozen ripples in the rivers
wind so strong
the water only wants to move
and move and move
but it is solid
interrupted in a moment of chaos
stuck like this until the calm
when the sun decides
to raise its voice

did you know the people are back
the ones who shout and scream in the night
sometimes i swear the voices are in my head
until i see the torch lights gleaming
good god
what if i've imagined the light, too

i can't believe anyone would dare
venture out in this bitter night
i walked in the frost-splintered breeze
for no more than two minutes
before giving in
my eyelids burned red
beaten raw from the snow
i tried so hard to endure

did you know
i have no one else to talk to, deirdre
no one at all

animal crossing

i lay down a beautiful rug
in front of the fire that never goes out
i make a banquet that i cannot eat
but its warmth brings me joy
and my home feels so full

i wear my fluffiest jumper
with my favourite lace-up boots
and the little snowman thanks me
for making him perfect
my neighbours tell me, wide-eyed,
that i disappeared for months
and it's good to see my face

i sit by the water and i watch
as the sky turns pink behind me
turns to purple
turns to black
fills with shooting stars
and i make a wish that i could stay
where the world is mine to build
and my mortgage is already paid
my god, it would be so easy
if there was nothing but this place

the daily ritual

the sky knocks against my window
and i respond to the calls
with a faux fur coat that poisons the seas
and boots made of something's skin
i walk the streets
well, just the one houseless road
rattling leaves and decaying blackberries
line my path and i call them my red carpet
because when there is nothing else
there is nothing else
and you do what you can because you must

and nobody sees me
in the outfit i picked out especially
for leaving the house
a little glitter on my eyes
not too much; the right amount for 4pm
lips glistening with whatever lipgloss is made of
hair clean; brushed
and nobody sees me
on this hollow road
the only road near me; the nothing
between two towns of almost nothing

finally, a car passes
and it's my mother
she has already seen me today
this outfit was built not to impress her,
but strangers
'need a lift?' she jokes
'ha,' i laugh

and she's gone
once again the road is quiet

i wish for a moment that i was in london
but right now
london probably isn't much busier
every main character with her perfect outfit
perfect hair and phone pressed to her ear
because she's a person who is busy and needed
has gone into hibernation
every person for me to look at
who once looked at me
in the fashion show that is the city
is not where i want them to be

the belly of every town has cooled
heartbeats slowed
the world has gone to sleep
i'm in a land of rain and grass and trees
pressed against the cold wet road
feeling for its pulse
and all i want is to be seen

it's only a meltdown

i am still here
but in liquid form
all of my worry and all of my peace
is now one
can't shake the fear off my joy
can't shake the joy off my fear
and when i weigh it all up
everything is equally as okay
as it is awful
and i think i can live with that
after all of the awful
plain awful all over and crying so much
the type of crying where
there's no real release
you feel sick and grey
(like a cloud that wants to disappear
but somehow it just can't
no matter how much it rains)
after all of this i think i can face
a bit of happiness
mixed in with a bit of pain

infinite august

in my dreams
it's august and i'm swimming
floating in circles
tuscan mountaintop spinning
the sun squints his eyes at us
sure we're up to no good
but he cannot deny
it feels glorious
sinking holy heads
beneath glistening blue
coming back up for air
and bread and wine
and laughter
lots of laughter
august in an infinity pool
come back to us
for you haven't always been
just a dream

the first gathering

embers dancing
hands holding
hope
among other things
chests bright
warm
laughing
golden hour sinking
and we'll be okay
we will be okay

i pulled a piece of lavender
from my pastel hair

and i looked like someone
who i always wished
i'd grow into

breathe the sky

wind, birds, sun
surround me infinitely
air feels sharp
belly in stitches
keep running
10 more seconds
quiet country roads
not a single car
music playing through earphones
flung over my shoulder
because i'd rather listen to the world
3, 2, 1
knees almost buckle
as i stop to catch my breath
but keep walking
don't stop moving
this is what we were made for
and i gave up my daily token
to be right here
still in lockdown but somehow free
out in the polite spring sun
creeping carefully day by day
unsure if we're ready for her
unaware of how deeply we love her
blue, green, golden
soak my gaze
the great outdoors coats me
and everything is okay

moss

where did you come from,
rootless thing?
dark damp green
you live here
      and
   there
earth's bodily growth
wanderer
so fresh and new
i want to touch you
flowerless thing
i'm infatuated
with the ground

bittersweet gifts

we'll remember the year
when everything was burning
places, animals, people
our chests
burned with rage
in the name of hate
in the name of love

we smashed the faces of every clock
who knows if it's march or july
never mind
being lost in the present
let us learn our past
build our future
break the concept of time
it never did us any good

we'll remember the year
when everything we knew died
when we learnt we are nothing more
and nothing less than what we put out
into the world
and there's a sweetness,
a goodness in being alive
if you allow it

things that feel good to write down

I. i got out of bed without thinking. without checking social media. without delay.

II. i moved my body until it dripped with sweat.

III. i sang to myself in my bedroom.

IV. i replied to those messages.

V. i dangled my legs out the window when it started to rain. reached my fingertips out. pressed droplets between them. i smiled at the purging sky.

VI. i told him, 'not now, i'm busy.'

VII. i touched the trees as i passed them by. i think i heard them breathing.

VIII. i tidied my room and the carpet thanked me for trying harder today than i did yesterday.

IX. i practiced latin. i enjoy learning a language i'll never have to speak so i don't have to feel shy about pronunciation.

X. i watered my plants. they reminded me that i need water to grow, too.

the light that comes and goes

i wonder why i cannot be okay all the time
the mirror reflects burning questions
onto my bare chest
or are they just smudges from greasy fingers
either way, they glow, and things that glow
often speak

why do i think about these things?
why do i dream of places that hurt?
why do i work so hard to be
the person i am fighting for
when she is going to break anyway?

i dyed my hair pink
like i wanted to at 17
i was too afraid back then
didn't feel strong enough
worry makes a person old
i am younger now than before
following instincts like i've got time
like everything is temporary
so i may as well test the limits
isn't it incredibly awful
that i spent my teenage years
stopping myself from doing what i liked?

i am her mother
building space for her dreams

to grow into freedom before responsibility
oh, to be in this time
the summer of graduation
studying is over and work is yet to begin

i am soaking up each day in all its beauty
every piece of the sky's falling goodness
but just like embers
the light fades when it touches the ground
some days i am the ground
others, i'm the trees
and on sacred days, the sea
i wish i could have more of those but honestly
it's been a painful week

the mirror glistens
from the light in my eyes
it is still there if you look closely
i couldn't see it
until i pulled a piece of lavender
from my pastel hair
and i looked like someone
who i always wished
i'd grow into

the planets of the men i've loved

venus in his eyes made me feel at home
while it was miles away
i had to break the chain
and realise it was not him i loved
but my own reflection

jupiter spun me round his finger
twirling and giggling
i thought i was having fun
until it stopped
and he left me dizzy

mercury brought me clouds
he told me their names, their shapes
made them tangible to me
but they were still clouds
and i still couldn't see

the sun was predictable
but in his face i was blind
glowing happily
serotonin high
hot hot hot until it burned

i learned the galaxy through people
with their godly hues and stardust voices
they taught me to look up
and believe in something bigger than me

but i taught myself that the galaxy is in me

the risk

of course i'm afraid
of meeting a stranger
from the internet
and getting murdered

i'm just more afraid
of dying alone

take me all the way

the way you open up the window//just a crack//your throat bobs so perfectly when you drink// take me to the moon just to say goodnight in a different light// we both know you're better than this//how soon is too soon to run//take me away from the awful sound//as far from here as we can go//you know the place//i love you there//but it can only ever be there//do you understand?

scar-pink

my head rises and falls in short bursts
atop your smoker's chest
and i wonder what your lungs look like
what hues our interlinked bodies are inside
and whose is winning

if your aching grey flesh has cast a shadow
across my clean pink lungs
or if, just like your outsides,
your insides are begging mine to fix them

i'm not all kindness to my body
(in a world like this,
who has never hurt themself?)
but while you clench and roar
scratch skin and grind teeth
i hold onto the survivor in me
wondering why we challenge our fleshy homes
race against the ticking clock of beating heart
poke and hurt and bully our living parts
while all they do is try
to keep us alive

i can say with certainty
write it on my grave
my chest has been brighter
since you went away
to all the men who hurt me
i damn well said goodbye
and your body is the worst thing
that ever happened to mine

yellow

find me in the mornings
sun-yellow
beneath the light of beginning
bitter, between conscious
and something else
does it make you feel godly
that you get to see me like this?
raw and plain
naked, honest
breath sour from the night
and all the places it took us
all the times we've lived and died
touch the smooth surface
of my waxwork body
if you're lucky i'll start to melt
my curves spilling slowly, like honey
and you'll sink into me
like a sleeping corpse
buried

leave the light on

for the sake of us
for the oath
not to stay the night
leave
we don't belong like this
the night is pulling
our stubborn limbs
light boils up
the bad in our bones
sin rises to the surface
we can see it so clearly
anyone could see it
but still
i lay you down
on your back
and we break every rule
we ever made

faux

how come your freckles taste like sugar
eyes glitter like you stole the sea
consumed it whole
with that sunshine-beating chest
how come your words keep on singing
for days and days
when you've walked away and forgotten
but still i'm searching
for any trace of you left for me to swallow

how come your freckles dissolve like sugar
your eyes glitter in artificial light
chest is warm just like the rest of us
and your words only linger when they're mean
how come i love you anyway
when your beauty is false
your heart is plain
and the only real part
is that you always, always leave

the sun is sinking

its teeth into the horizon
i watch as the day dies
like all that came before it

crossing my fingers
tight like shoelaces
hoping and begging
that the haunting will go away
and i won't have to set any fires

i do not want to be
a person who destroys things
quiet daydreamer
artist, poet
all my life i've been told
i was born to create
and i never wanted
to break anything

i wonder if the sun feels the same
for each day it gives, it takes one away
creeps up on the night
kills it at the crack of dawn
just to thrive for a while
before sinking again
the sun dies a million times
and all it does is glow
but all it does is burn

the game

so you come back for the hell of it
to ask me how i've been
to make me cry one more time
like it's nothing
like you could do it in your sleep

and i think
or i thought
i had stopped loving you
but i still do not know
how to see your name
pop up on my phone
and not reply

and while i think
i have moved on
i still don't know
how to sleep at night
because there you were
existing right by me
and now i lay corpse-like
through the dark hours
wondering why
with all of my heart
all my living parts
i could not be enough

and i don't know what you want me to say
when you filled my world with stars
poured them down my throat
like a glittering wine
until your tricks began to look
so much like hope

we will never want the same things
we are not like the dying plant
i almost threw away
who suddenly found her colour
and began reaching up
like she could touch the sky
maybe she will someday
but not us

we are not a shrivelled thing
with a chance of growing
we are a waste of everything that we are
don't you see that i'm tired?
this is a dirty, hopeless game
i don't want to play anymore

morning swim

like bubbles rising to the top of a glass
of sweet champagne,
the sun comes up

above the waves
their tingling salt water breath
bitter to the taste

you hold your head above the water
take in the sunrise on bare skin
the sea wrecks your hair

but it doesn't matter
because you're awake
you know this because you're afraid

and that's okay
some hearts are hard-wired to race
it's okay

of all the crumbling shipwrecks on this beach
you are the most alive
and that is freedom

if nothing else
you are free

we, the crisis

the earth has been burning
for longer than we have
our chests ache till we're numb
we live and we die
we live and we die
and someday we'll all be dead
and the world will have a better shot at life
than it ever did with us

the more you think,
the harder it is to breathe
and i wonder how i ever manage without trying
they say focus on your breathing
to find your calm
but i've never felt more scattered

i think you're lying when you say my name
like how my laughter is false
but you don't mind it
you like the sound of me
and i like the way you breathe

i used to think we as a species
will easily have another billion years here
now i wonder if we'll make it out of this life
at old age or if we'll burn with the rest of them
and there will be no one left to bury us

i hope you're next to me when it happens
when we run out of chances
i hope you're my last one

guy fawkes, 2020

my heart beats fast with joy, not anxiety//a pitter patter like rain, not a dizzying thump//my heart skips//like a child in the woods collecting sticks for the bonfire//the finest i can scavenge//thorns catch in my hair and tear my clothes//and i pull through// like where i'm going matters more than how i look// later i pull a stick from the edge of the fire//in a pocket of heat and glowing coals i set it alight//and play with the flames like the good old days//

when playing with fire was not sagittarian heartbreaks at 3am//but lingering on the edge of nature's bared teeth//learning to trust and fear it at once//comfort and excitement licking the air//i pick marshmallow strings from my apple-round cheeks//and this is the most i have smiled since i was a little girl//i wonder if joy is not only attached to my age//but to the ways i brought wonder into my life when i was her//

maybe i'm sad because i'm 23//lost and exhausted and empty of love//but maybe i could learn from the girl with twigs in her knotted hair//sticky cheeks and moss-stained clothes//wrapped in blankets and laughing, really laughing//because she was happy.
i was happy.

kensington

bodies glide in a metal tube
overground, a million views
and i'm in love with this city
i love it over and over every time i come back
attaching, detaching, reattaching
the longest on-off relationship i've ever known

think of all the pollution in that black-grey air
but in the clouded smoker's chest of london
my skin has never been clearer

an elderly woman shouts into her phone
vulgar in a foreign language
she has no shits to give
i sit across from her, reading

in bed, i hear sirens
they don't frighten me here
streets filled with drunken fights, heart attacks
but the cars are singing
we'll make it better
and as i fall asleep, i believe them

a woman in a cafe serves a hundred people a day
but she remembers my order every time

children scream through holland park
so i go house-spotting on the pretty streets
pink blossoms from rare trees
fall into my hair like i belong here
and i'll try to belong here

dear pre-covid lover

we haven't talked since before everything
november streets, hand holding
pedestrian crossing buttons
pressed with bare fingers, not through sleeves
back when you could learn a person
by watching their lips as they speak

now we look in strangers' eyes from a distance
wonder if their eyebrows were always so expressive
or if it's 2020's evolution
forcing connection with someone
who can't see who you are
every shy voice raised louder than ever

it's not all bad, really
i've been doing okay through all this
early mornings, new rituals
not that you really asked
i think we all quit asking,
how've you been?
when the default answer changed
from *good, thanks* to *well, you know*

we met before the masquerade
when every sea of strangers
became a sea of danger
every creature painted bad
by the tainted air around them

and in this new world
where the old is forgotten,
never to return
i'm not sure what to say to you
after all this
i'm not sure we know each other
anymore

dear Not God

invisible shapeless thing
it's not that i believe in you
but i believe in everything i've seen
and if tiny little earth can hold so much
i wonder what else there might be
beyond the playground
of our own infinity

through the eyes of you
or some other impossible thing
i wonder what i look like
if i'm even seen
i know the stars burn hot like the sun
but they shine so peacefully from down here
the stars and i, we're made of the same stuff
tell me how far apart we need to be
for me to shine like that

to look like anything but this
human creature thing
        we are awfully strange
so loud and dangerous
        for something so weak
but it's true that everything looks ugly
when you get too close
maybe that's why they made you invisible

my last tinder date

you stop me in my tracks
and we're beside hyde park
between my fingers, your fingers
between this pavement and the other,
a hundred speeding cars pass us
like we're just two people
you smile like we're not broken
and i almost
believe you

the moon tracks us down
i can't count on my fingers
the times she's caught us
when i reach my hand inside your chest,
your heartbeat is speeding like my touch
is the flight you're afraid you're gonna miss
but you made the airport just in time and it's okay
that the engine is broken because i am the engine
and we both knew i'd bring you down with me

this poem is the beginning of the end

when i opened my eyes

it was still dark
and i was afraid of my own breathing
like it   or i   could hurt you
in my little human state of waking
fleshy   born
                        dangerous
i think you are the crime i commit
you are my final move
in the game i never liked
but had to play

because no one is any good at all
until they're naked
and picked apart from themselves
like old wallpaper

i opened my eyes to the sinking dread
that you were going to leave
and i gripped you tighter

if i am afraid of how i feel
then you should be, too

a map of invisible things

visions
of us
so clear, i could've sworn–

but no
the air between us
grows heavier

fogs up the glass
of who we were

our love is buried now

were you even listening?

i loved you
till our love was dead

are you there?

were you somewhere else
the whole time?

both, leaving

sugar-sweet fingertips on his skin
like they're hungry
mouth open, just a little
eyes adoring, all over
he feels the honey-glazed warmth
of something he wasn't ready for

cocooned like two baby-somethings in spring
he leaves his own bed while she's in it
door open and the air on his face
her kisses floating away
with the smoke spilled from his tired lungs
his heart doesn't know it yet
but it's such a shame

a month in almost-heaven
after so many locked away
the world said *ready or not, here i come*
nervous footsteps out of overgrown doors
and the first arms he fell into were hers
she was never the world before all of this happened
but she is now

and when he crawls back
into the bed she made neatly for him
with his clothes folded, chair pushed in
she'll be nowhere to be found

maybe i'm just dehydrated but

i feel vaguely unwell
sort of weak
and grey
tepid rain on tired glass panes
the creatures
in the woodlands
of my fading mind
find shelter in the trees
from summer
giving up on itself

i thought by now
i would be waking
from my wintery self
alive with longing
to throw my wriggling body
into that sea
like a school of minnows
zipping cluster of energy

am i no longer august?
what has become
of the ocean in me?
is it this city
away from the coast
or the sun that hides the moon
she who throws me in
makes waves of me

where is the siren that sings?
has she forgotten me?

my house says to me:

my dear,
why don't you live here anymore?
i know the world was broken
and you had to stay
but when you were allowed to leave
you didn't really have to go
don't you know that?
you could've stayed here
where you were happy and safe
when home felt like home
and your things and your smells
were right where they belonged
now you come back and you're different
your gaze fogged with grey
and your clothes just don't smell right
and i know it's still you, of course it is
but you left
and we fell out of love
and you haven't found yourself anywhere else
you hold your head high
like you know who you are
but when you come back to me
and you're crying in the dark
i can see it all, my dear
you're becoming this girl
londoner with the hard shell
hiding in a made-up self
and i know
you despise her

sonder

stranger,
you've felt unimaginable things
you've been to places
i will never go
you've loved
you've said goodbye
and i'll never know why

you've thought the worst thought
you can possibly think of
you've wondered what would happen
if you smashed that window
if you stepped out into that road
if you screamed
at the top of your lungs
in a stranger's face
you've laughed your loudest
you've felt your heaviest

and i will never know you
maybe i wouldn't want to
but isn't it sad
that we go through life
with all this unknowing?
oh, i'm being silly
maybe it isn't sad at all
i don't care about you
you don't care about me
shall we just
leave it at that?

time

in the space between now
and forever
i fall into bed
like dust
i have already lived this day
but it has come again
because the days do as they please
and i will never understand
how time can be slow like a bruise
and faster than the fall
how pain beats like an eternal pulse
and laughter rots like petals
and nothing ever stays
but everything lingers
time is running out
is overflowing
is everywhere
i can't catch it
and i can't escape it

shiny broken thing

first
my voice went away
didn't make a dramatic exit
nor was there any sort of final straw
it just slowly
but surely
left

then it was my hands
the ones i use for all my trying
they just dropped off
crawled away beneath the desk
and i cannot get them back
without their help

my heart changed its pattern
when my limbs froze up
like if this body isn't trying
then this ribcage isn't worth it
and there are other chests
it would rather be beating in

and i don't think i'm beyond repair
i think i'm 20-something
and i'm angry because who wouldn't be
and i keep letting pieces of me die
because i don't blame anything
for giving up on me while i'm like this

i hope i'm not always like this
for the sake of whatever is left of me

i've seen how my broken parts
glitter in the light
when i'm shattered on the floor
at least i'm pretty
at least i look like something
that might've been worth something
a long time ago

but unless the love of my life
turns out to be a magpie
i'll probably die alone

burning building

like a match, like a secret
a room full of dust
i burn

like bodies, like skin
paper-thin wings
photos on the walls
hanging, lifeless
memories on a string

like groins and chests
cuts and fevers
i burn i burn i burn

everything turned to nothing
woman, vision, whisper
thing, smoke, gone

and the flames
are so
quiet

you wouldn't notice at all
if i wasn't the brightest light
this glowing city
has ever seen

pretty little things

flowers are growing at the sides of roads
and they're all a dead person who someone loved
people die at the sides of roads
flowers grow from dead bodies
and people love you even when you die
when your skin sinks into your skull
and your blood has stopped
and your blood is gone
people love you still
you're the life bursting through the dirt
through the sad cold concrete
the ground mourns in petals
your strange parts rot
flesh disappears
the earth will grow to love you
and this is the worst thing we will ever be
just human, just breathing
just morning breath and terrible singing
and buying the bread with the later use by date
even though the older bread
would also have been fine
when we die
we won't be these silly little things
ugly little things
look at the flowers at the side of the road
look at those
pretty little things
and that's what we'll be someday
that's what we'll be

this is how we learn
that happiness
is a thing we create
and this world
is full of it

are you happy?

is this the dream?
me, your world
the one you always longed for
another sky and another moon
somehow more beautiful
than anything before
are you happier than ever?
like every day is the first?
will you tell me i'm good?
every day, like you mean it
like i'm the sea and the stars
and you could never wish
for anything more
are you happy?

the question

a month before we risked it all
i asked a friend,
if you had to choose someone
who you already know
and marry them tomorrow
who would you choose?
the friend said,
i don't have an answer for that
i told them i would choose you
easily
that i have always known
that it's not like i'm in love with you
no, not at all
i just know it would work
that i loved you once
six years ago
that i have moved on
a dozen times
and it's been fine, sure
but they never came close
never filled that void
my 18-year-old self
was far wiser than i am now
she knew love when she saw it
and i still wallow in the regret
of never trying
and my friend said,
that's pretty weird, man
you should probably talk to him

ours

summer skies like crimson at dawn
silken rocks glisten
bodies dripping wet
sweet like citrus
on your tongue
my body on yours
sea salt hair
down our backs
look at those waves
so gentle
in these moments i swear
the sea has never been angry
when our bodies breathe together
i swear we've never hated a thing
you're not the only tide
this moon has pulled
but you're the only one i trust
with my opal skin
mermaid lungs
and my whole heart
tonight is only ours

undying

okay but so what if nothing is forever
and no matter how many pinky promises
we make in moonlit streets
we will lose each other to something
so what?
if i can see myself love you
before it's even happened
and i see our love so big
it'll light the skies so bright
the sun and the moon will simply leave
because they're no longer needed
and so what if everything
finally ends up perfect
and then you die?
well then
i'll never run out of ways
to brag about how good it was
to be loved by you
hell, give me a challenge
make me list the ways
you made me laugh myself to sleep
i'll never run out
make me list the ways
you made my anger dissolve like sugar
i'll never run out
make me list the ways
and i'll have a fun little game
to last me the rest of forever
if, god forbid, our forever
gets cut short

this goodness? we made it

your moon-glowing face
my grateful hands holding it
us, like soft petals
tender, thin-skinned
bruised and torn
but still pure
still us
and i kiss the edge of your chin
and we still remember the day we met
but we hold onto this one
we hold onto you and i
skin on skin
the same lights twinkling
arms around my waist
face pressed into my neck
we are golden
and this is how we learn
that happiness is a thing we create
and this world is full of it

the astronaut

if i believed in god
i'd like to think
he's an astronaut

sailing through space
replacing bulbs in flickering stars
and fanning the sun
when the summer heat
gets too much even for her

and when the moon gets restless
he sings lullabies
so her waves down on earth
don't crash too hard
on our beaches

and he orders a rainfall
a week in advance
just in time to save our crops
but mainly because
he likes the heavy clouds
likes to let them out
to play sometimes

and when he put you and i
together by chance
we were his favourite accident
and when he reads this poem
he'll say
what a load of rubbish

sunday morning

skin on skin
holding each other
in eternal arms
him in my bed
me in his bed
soon we'll have one
that is ours
and a million mornings
just like this
bodies singing
souls intertwined
we should get up
i'm getting up
okay now i mean it
oh, babe, fine
just one more hour
and i want to live
all of my lives
just like this
with him

shoebox

i cried when i moved in here
after isolation went on so long
that the madness turned into safety

i no longer belonged in the city
scared of stepping out my door
landing on a busy high street
or escaping to the local park
and finding it riddled with tourists
the kind i used to be

returning to this little room
with barely a crack of floor space
a neighbour's bathroom window
as my only view
and i thought at least i'm alone
if tight spaces do one thing well
it's the illusion of comfort
with only walls wrapped around you

but we fell in love in this room
we found a way to make it feel
bigger than it was
and we filled it up
with so much more than it could hold

it's bittersweet to let it go
we'll have other homes, you and me
but this is where it started
and that has to count
for something

illusion

a lover who doesn't leave me
crying on my birthday
who holds me like something
he never wants to lose

who never tires of a pretty sunset
look at that sky!
who finds beauty everywhere
and somehow
he chose me

tucked between our sheets
in our bed
asking if i've got
any tiktoks to show him
and i say yes
he lays his head on my chest
and i can't believe
this is my life
i can't believe it

limbs

the   luxury   of   having
both   mine   and   yours
    enough   body
to   get   tangled
    twisted   trunk
        branches
        reaching   out
    all our separate parts
    waving   hello
        to april   sun
    my leaves shiver
    against yours
        your   bones
    warm my bones
    our tangled branches
    one   shared   trunk
        we are everything
    that   grows

us, drifting

in dreams
we are still the same
you (hottest sun)
me (summer rain)
our sleeping limbs
always searching
for each other

but if i was gone
if something like heaven
missed me too much
i hope you would find me

in the creaking
of trees i used to climb
in forget-me-not sprinkles
on the ground
in cardigan sleeves
dog-eared pages
and in every corner of spring
i hope you find me

because when we lay here
scattered like constellations
in our separate wanderings
we meet again in every dream
and i love you
even when we're asleep

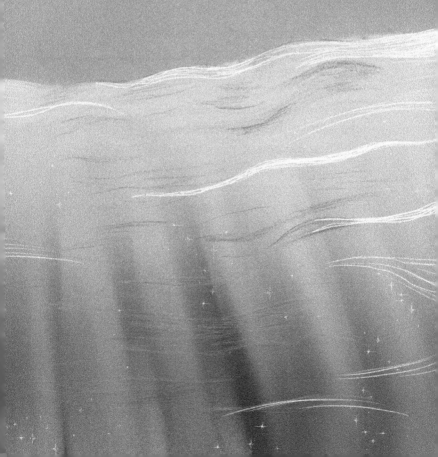

as if it's all you were made for

and all you'll ever know

you live

my hometown is a museum

my hometown is a museum
of first kisses and cigarettes
shared with people who no longer live here

a walking tour of every curb that scraped my knee
every cheap coffee
every friend i thought i'd never lose

it seems odd that i went to boarding school
five minutes away from my house
my two homes side by side, holding hands

but to me it is stranger being back here
without the faces i grew up with
the kebab shop trips at 11pm

sitting in the harsh light in our school hoodies
talking about the future and wondering
how life could ever be more than this

and honestly, i'm not sure it is
but maybe that's okay and maybe we were right
when we said all we needed was each other

my childhood friends may never all be
in the same place at the same time again
but as long as i am here

this town won't forget their footsteps

places i have cried

a public toilet
on the phone wondering
where the hell i went wrong
in your bed
in my bed
while you sleep
while you watch, silent
the train home
the train away from home
deep in the night
where no one can see
a bathtub in tuscany
trying to suck the tears back in
don't let a pointless man
ruin time with good friends
i'm fine i'm fine i'm fine
brave face
the starbucks at liverpool street
because i don't have 30p
to hide in the toilets
colchester station, lost
mid-breakup
waiting for my dad to pick me up
in the kitchen
in my mother's arms
on the floor with the dogs
apple-round cheeks
laughing
as they lick away the tears
perfect places, terrible places
i cry wherever i please

poets bathe in melancholy

have you found yourself yet?
in a stranger's bedroom
reborn   between foreign sheets
or wasting in the damp
on your own sad ceiling?

have you found a way to be?
     really be
like the plants in poundland
that continue to grow
because they are plants
and that is what they do

and like me with the words
i don't write every day but when i do
i know it is why i breathe
and you swore you hated your job
swore you'd quit tomorrow
drive right out of this life
into a new one

five years on
where are you?

i knew who i was
where my life belonged
but there was a time
when i wished you'd take me with you
when i'd have left my own life
for your unknown path
that i believed sacred

we will never know each other again
your life will never matter to mine
but wherever you were going
i hope you got there
despite everything

the healing that will come

you let me down easy
and by easy, i mean i fall
like it's all i was made to do

a glass ornament
that always lived too near
the edge of the coffee table
aiming for the rug
but finding itself shattered
between the cracks in the hardwood floor

an avalanche
the rain on my window
i've fallen so far already
but still the only way is down

you drop me quicker
than you dropped my hand
the time we saw her in the street
all along the answer
was never going to be me

i am pouring
against your windscreen
so i am all you see
i'm prickling your toes
in the bed you share with her
and you're reminded of all
the broken shards of me

we're only 16
you don't know how to forget
what you did to me
but time will wash it away
you'll be fine long before i am
but the cracks in my chest will fill in
and i'll know you had to break me
so you could hold her more carefully
it may never feel fair
but it will feel okay anyway

and when i'm 25 i will have nothing
but good things to say about you

the danger of living

is that anything could happen
and look what's happened

all of the good
all of the bad
time is not a line
but a growing thing
that keeps building on
to your old dead self

every smile,
the birth of new lines

every scar,
the death of a wound

to live
is the most lethal thing
we could ever do

but we stay anyway
breathing while we know
someday it will stop

laughing when life is funny
because other times it is sad

touching each other
weeding the garden
feeding the cat, hugging the cat

watching the trees
how they move an awful lot
for such stationery things
every branch dancing
with every breeze

as if it's all you were made for
and all you'll ever know

you live

garden

it's spring
my mother is baking
and my father
is in the garden
pulling weeds
making room
for new things to grow
the dogs are so peaceful
laying in the sun
eyelids heavy
the cat examines a pile
of freshly pulled weeds
in the paddock
new lambs are skipping
over the road
fields are humming
thick with yellow
heavy scent
my mother decorates
a chocolate meringue
with mini eggs
i am here
and what a place
to exist

little cottage

when the rain has stopped
the trees keep on crying
just in case
there is something left
to mourn

my shoulders
catch the damp of droplets
slipping from above
as the leaves shed their weight

and when the sun pricks the clouds
they burst right open
      like new wounds
and the world
      is so far away
but it is still right there
at the foot of the bed

and i can't wait
to touch it

suffolk skies

i'm home and the sky isn't blue
it's pink and golden
and it's screaming with life
red cuts through mauve
cuts through violet

the sun kisses this town
so hard
that we won't forget it
when it goes down

i'm home and the sky is dancing
like suffolk missed me
more than i could know
i take it in
and like the clouds
my soul
feels so much lighter

if a star can be a fish

then the oceans
must light up
a billion times
from the sky
and our world
must look
so impossible

                              if a forest can be a fire
                              then the earth
                              greatest mother
                              must have an alter ego
                              she didn't tell us about

if a kiss can be goodbye
then love must be
a trick of the eye
and we'd rather stay here
and we'd rather be blind

                              if a wound can heal
                              then pain is everything
                              pain is nothing
                              and that's a whole lot
                              of cells that won't stop
                              being reborn

and you are made
of a billion little
don't give ups

acknowledgements

Thank you to my family for always encouraging me to do all the silly little things I want, like writing these poems.

Thank you to those who provided support and feedback throughout the development of this book: Felix, Harry, Hayley, John, Joshua, Liza, Mark, Michael and Toby.

Thank you to Emma for all your guidance and support during this project, and throughout my Publishing MA.

Thank you to the lovely authors who wrote such kind early reviews and described this book far better than I could've done: Hannah Cao, Hannah Murray, Jennie Louise, Kristiana Reed, Liam Xavier and Olivia Snowdrop.

Thank you to the poetry community on Instagram for continuing to lift me up and for giving me the confidence to share my work.

credits

Dear Pre-Covid Lover was first published in *Ripple 2022: A Student Anthology* (2022) by Kingston University Press.

The Planets of the Men I've Loved, *The Light that Comes and Goes* and *Bittersweet Gifts* were first published in *The Planets of the Men I've Loved* (2020) by Sunday Mornings at the River.

also by Jasmine S. Higgins:
A Girl is a Shapeshifter (2019)

Author photo © Joshua Higgins

Jasmine S. Higgins is a poet and hopeful future novelist based in London. She's been writing since she was about the size of her cat (very small) and hasn't used a capital letter since 2014 except for very important things like emails and this author bio. She has a BA in Fine Art and an MA in Publishing, both from Kingston University. Her first book *A Girl is a Shapeshifter* came out in 2019, and her second book *Mermaid Lungs* came out in 2022. She hosts a writing challenge with daily prompts under the hashtag #PromptsByJasmine on Instagram.

Lightning Source UK Ltd.
Milton Keynes UK
UKHW011020150822
407320UK00001B/102